High Shelf VII

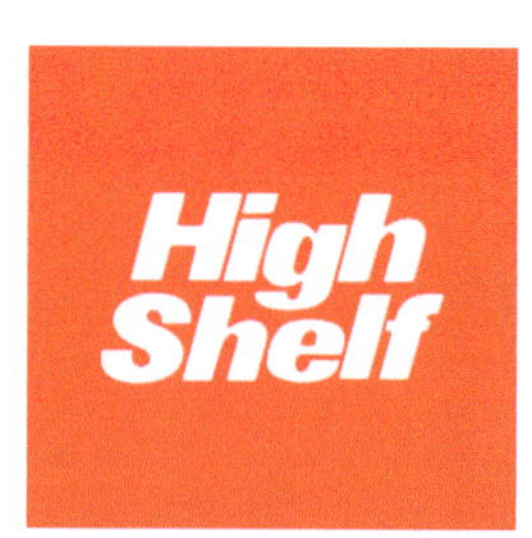

High Shelf Issue VII 1.7.19
Portland, Oregon.
Copyright 2019, High Shelf Press

ISBN: 978-1-7330279-2-2

Cover Image by Matt Gold
Design and Layout by C. M. Tollefson
Edited by Angela Dribben & C. M. Tollefson

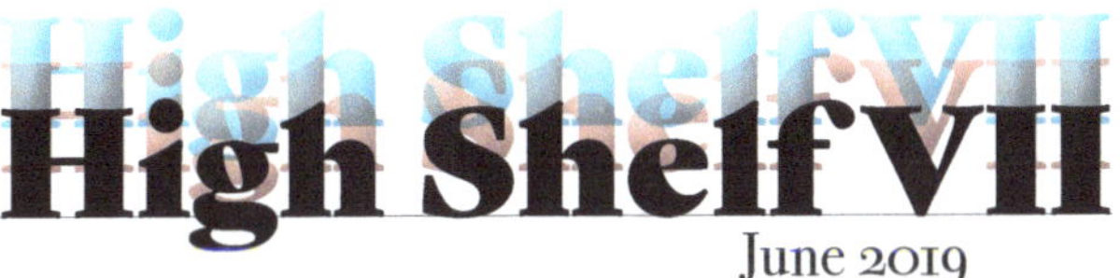

High Shelf VII

June 2019

"To the one she shared the citrus with but
never peeled together

...Nor resuscitate a bike tire while the other watched
or took the time to address
and unpaper all the cuts..."
Kat Schwartz

"...the wind howls around corners
like the heavy moan
of a deep nightmare..."
Ginny Short

Table Of Contents

Check-Up

Andreas Fleps

Well, doc,
my groin is in severe, sharp pain,
and my testicles are tender,
but I think it's because life
is a gigantic, prolonged shot
to the nuts, and hope is
existential blue balls.

My abdomen hurts also,
which means my heart
must have dropped from my chest
like an ancient angry asteroid,
and where it landed
there's unimaginable trauma;
a miles long pit in my stomach.

Nausea?
Just the need to throw up
my own name.

Chronic headaches?
No one ever told me there are thoughts
that can concuss from the inside.

The annoying muscle twitches?
My soul tapping the inside of my body,
asking to get out.

Unremitting diarrhea?
Well, I am stumped on that one,
though when you spend all your time on the toilet,
it's no wonder you view life as
shit.

The diagnosis is quite simple
as Beckett suggests:
I am on earth,
and there's no cure for that.

Being human is unhealthy,
and having skin is a death sentence.

The Day the Final Mermaid Died

Brynn Bogert

—after Kai Cheng Thom

I was plumbing at home   listening to the news

& the gross heaving grease smell   of what my sink had to say

& that day it felt like everything was curdling

& I could almost feel my apartment breaking   like a plate shifting   out to sea

& I guess, I missed her

& I wanted to see her silver skin

& scales, the harpoon scars defiant on her side   one more time

& all along the gross coastline birds   were limping like little fists   punching the dirt
        digging for carrion covered by breeze covered   by maggots covered   by my
        own   not looking

& I knew I was getting close though   because I heard her   not song   I
        heard the gas leaking from her gills

& I saw her lovely tons of flesh   splayed on the shore   her breasts gigantic
        transparent   brine-bubbled skin   her whale-eyes gooey   blinking

& beautiful in the unfiltered light of the beach

& she looked at me   at a pail that sat in the sand

& I began to scuttle across the beach   to splash water on her gills

& I gathered gallon, gathered   gallon, gathered whole spilled   swimming pools

& what splashed on my dress   burnt off   left a crab crust of salt-shell

o

& I had loved her growing up   had her image   maybe more doll-like   on every
        surface of my room

& I would finger the walls looking for water   looking for the coral would   run my
        fingers across my own legs   hoping for a splinter of scales

& across my lap   looking for some flat slickness   I do not have &
I loved her for looking like that &   eating sailors &   sinking their ships into the
          fat soup   of her hunger

                                                    o

& that day on the beach   my clothes kept cracking   for her

& blisters   nearly like gnarled coral calcified   my knuckles

& all the two of us could do was wait   for the frustrating tide

& hours after   high tide hadn't helped   her body just wedged there   like a mottled
          log

& there was nothing I wanted to do except spit   on it   for having asked   for having
          that awful fish-feathered body   like the kind I have

& I   I wanted so badly to lick   the salt-breath from those lips   for myself   I
          wanted to   kiss   until the pink skin of her   gums receded   leaving pearls
          inlaid with bones

& one huge corpse to dismantle by saw

& haul away   I wanted to display my own ship-sinking anger   which I had learned
          from watching her   battling bait from the boats

& taking hook in fin

& then   as if she sensed what I was thinking   she slammed her fish-limbs
          on the land
& said in a voice   so tired &   oiled &   clogged

Thank you I will

miss you   all along.

Alicia

Christine Alexander

A charmed life, solid-like:

Apple, piano, white teeth, French braid

Turning backbends in the backyard.

Spotting mine, smirking.

White on a wall is not white but

Bone and Ivory.

Eyelet, not lace

No crinoline or miniatures.

"Who wants to fuck Chrissy and Alicia?" Fifth grade and all the sixth-grade boys

raised their hands.

I didn't know what that meant but I knew it was something good. I wanted to
shriek or link arms, but we weren't that kind of friends. She swallowed her smile,
and we walked fast past the boys, Alicia with her cool gray stare

Not gray. Stone or Smoke. Graphite? Ash.

But later, sixteen, I heard things:

"She was on top then I guess she, like, leaned back. How slutty is that?"

Backbends.

I could picture it, showing off like doing penny drops,

Knees hooked around the metal rungs,

rocking until she rocketed up and over,

Perfect landings always.

This new savage thing- this I wanted to see

A hitch in the hips, a slip

The sloppiness of wanting.

Domestic Musicality

Kevin Edwards

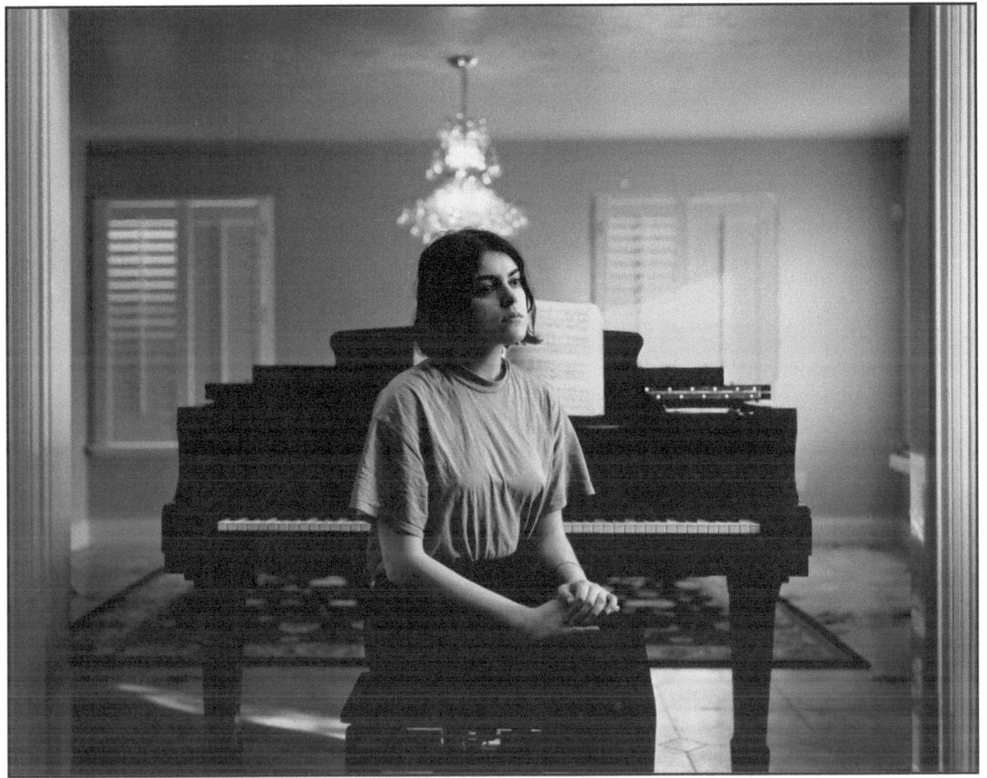

COSMOLOGY 33

Alison Lubar

I. Weaving Prophecy
you pull me back into myself,
phantom mending golden filament:
vision revised through delphic swirls of melted ice in rye,
within the curled rims of paper coffee cups.

II. Summer Arbor
transformed new and foreign
my every petal shivers,
       even leaves mistake you in moonlight for the sun.

III. Open, as
a letter, tulip, porch door,
the row between chorus girls
the space between trees and stars.

IV. Quotidian Knowing
where your sneakers wear out,
your Sunday afternoon self,
milk to cereal ratio:
       this is how I will treat the symptoms,
       measured in slotted spoons.

V. A Stranger
       Once, when this almost happened,
like the *pied noir* awaiting his execution,
       I felt ready to live it all again.

VI. Tragic Marginalia
When will you slip to the periphery,
surrender to an endnote? How will I survive
the scatter of cells, syllables? How will I survive
       this dispersion,
       the soul's diaspora?

VII. New Ontology
I believe in
       concrete geometry
       over destructive mythologies:
the intersection of two lines, not on a flat graph,
       but rather a sphere, fated to meet each year:
       two points of contact, numerically distinct,
       equidistant and infinite collision.

The earth is good for this.

WINDWARD

Ginny Short

--Spring Wind 2018

stand with me here under the night-moth moon

> the wind cuts like the shiver
> of glaciers calving
> in a distant sea

we'll listen for the sound of the heart breaking

> the wind sinks deeply
> into my pores
> like bones in la brea tar

all we ever wanted was light-filled space

> the wind howls around corners
> like the heavy moan
> of a deep nightmare

there is only sadness hovering in the air tonight

> the wind sifts softly
> like drifting petals
> of jacaranda snow

East of Snowville

Violet Knight

if it could not be seen, then there was nothing. headlights pierced the black prairie like a bullet. the moon refused to shine—if it blinked it would be consumed by the black prairie & sucked into the charcoal vortex that stole birds from their bushes & rodents from their holes. the motor whistled like a panicked bat. torn guardrails jutted their jags toward the road like thumbs. mountainous spines drowned stars in shadow. as sleep chewed my eyes i heard utah hiss.

Phonography

Matt Gold

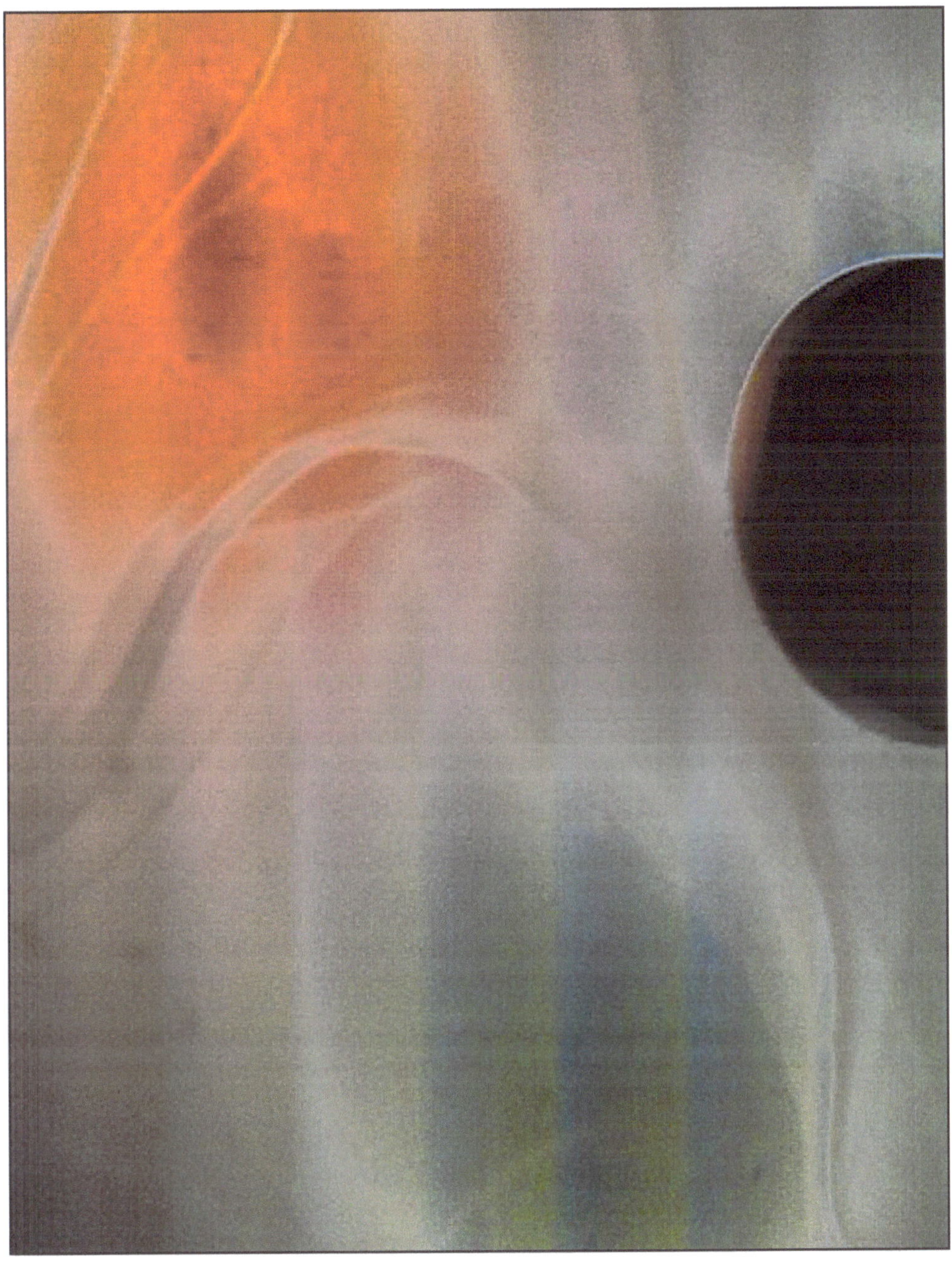

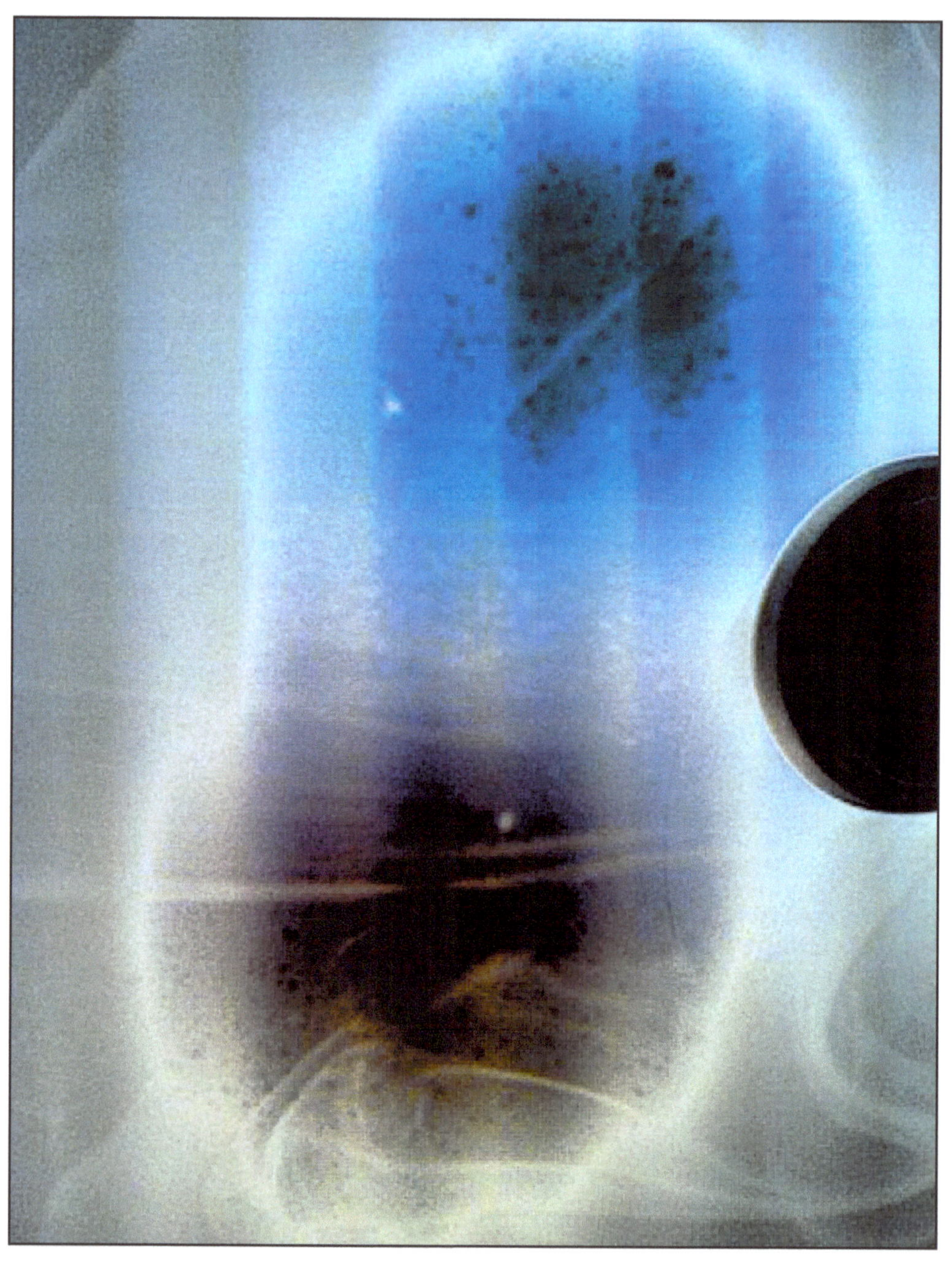

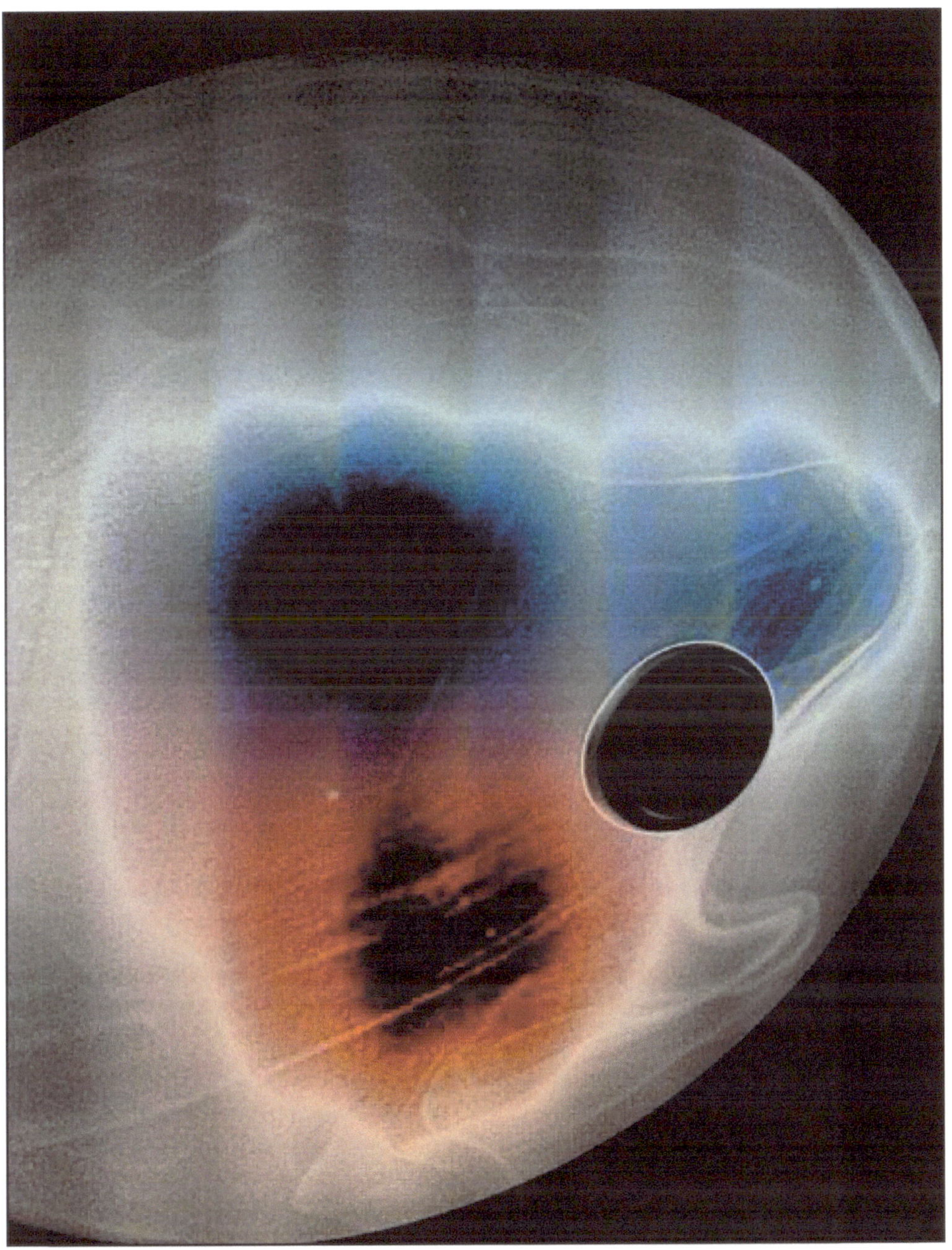

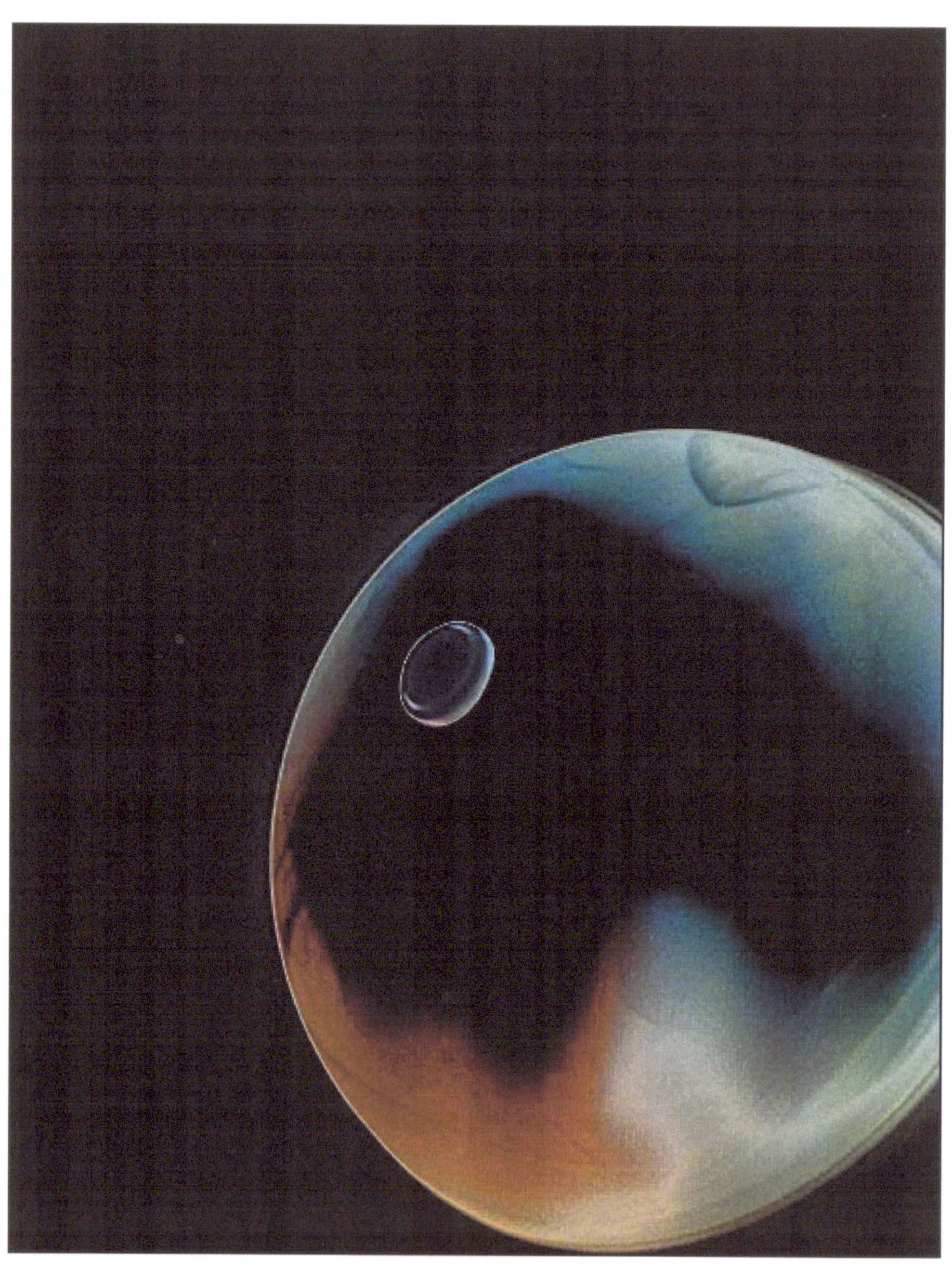

Sylvia Segmented

Paul Iasevoli

Oh what a thrill...of pink fizz
this is for Plath
as words rip
through her consciousness

leading her to Yeats' oven
to blow out the pilot
and suck death into her being
and let go as crows flow

like her husband's poetry
that yields despair
where no blue skies fly
over London's semidetached

while she disconnects
birthday joys and holidays
from effervescent yews'
bristling flowers

pollinating
with a million sperm
falling into water
where fish spawn

bubbling with love
and infidelities

in nightmare dreams
of dying children

and lost reams
of black confetti.

Wake of December

Riley Fields

I raked all of the leaves in the front yard today
and left body bags filled with Autumn
at the edge of the driveway.
When I came inside with heavy arms and frozen tears,
you were still gone.
And so I called you, after I pulled the thorns
from the backs of my thighs to tell you
I am sorry for the way the seasons
have changed things,
for the things we threw away
with only the bare winter ground
to show for it.

Disclosure/Concealment XXXIV

Planta Artis Reeder

23

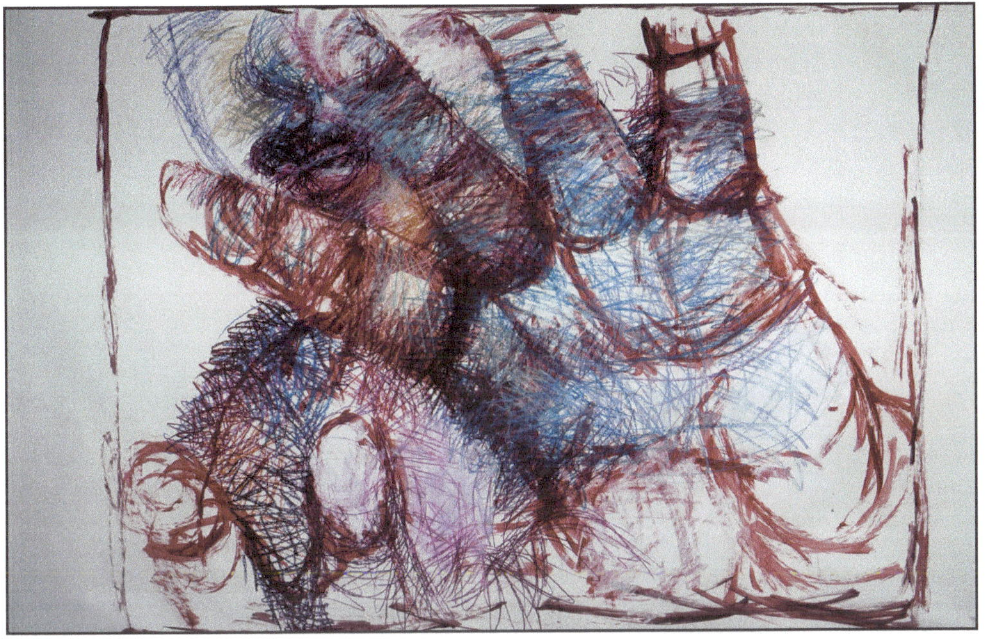

The Philosophy of Citrus

Kat Schwartz

To the one she shared the citrus with but
never peeled together

Nor sit beneath a humming willow and ask why it wept
or behold the phenomenon of fingers curling back the curls while they slept
and show them the tattoos
on the top right, middle (both sides), down to the bottom left

Nor pet praise the soft sweaters
only to shed them off
and giggle about her pronunciation of *Knuffel Kont*
beneath sun lit circus tent covers
or spill the orange juice side by side on a shared kitchen counter

Nor resuscitate a bike tire while the other watched
or took the time to address
and unpaper all the cuts
or share the knowledge of the day, the clementines at the market for instance
but at no extra tuition cost

Nor fix the bowtie before the family debacle
or suggest the worthy wrong noun for the crossword puzzle
and bring the cough drops and salted water
when the day before the sky drizzled

Nor place a calla lily in their hand
and ask to describe the scent
or see them wink at the sun and know exactly what they meant
and wonder how NASA had been so terribly mistaken,
because there were never that many stars before they met, not even five
yet alone one hundred billion

Nor debate the way the moon got its bruises
and ask her what it was she truly wanted:
if it was
faster or slower?
the pandemonium or the silence?
the heavens of Pablo Neruda or the walls of Shakespeare's sonnets?

Nor split the grapefruit in half to kiss it back to whole
or throw consideration out the window
so they could let the ashes go up
and jump the gun to
take the leap
and inquire about what it was across a neon green bicycle
and choose the honorable risk,
even if it didn't end in a we

Nana's Hands

Kayla Branstetter

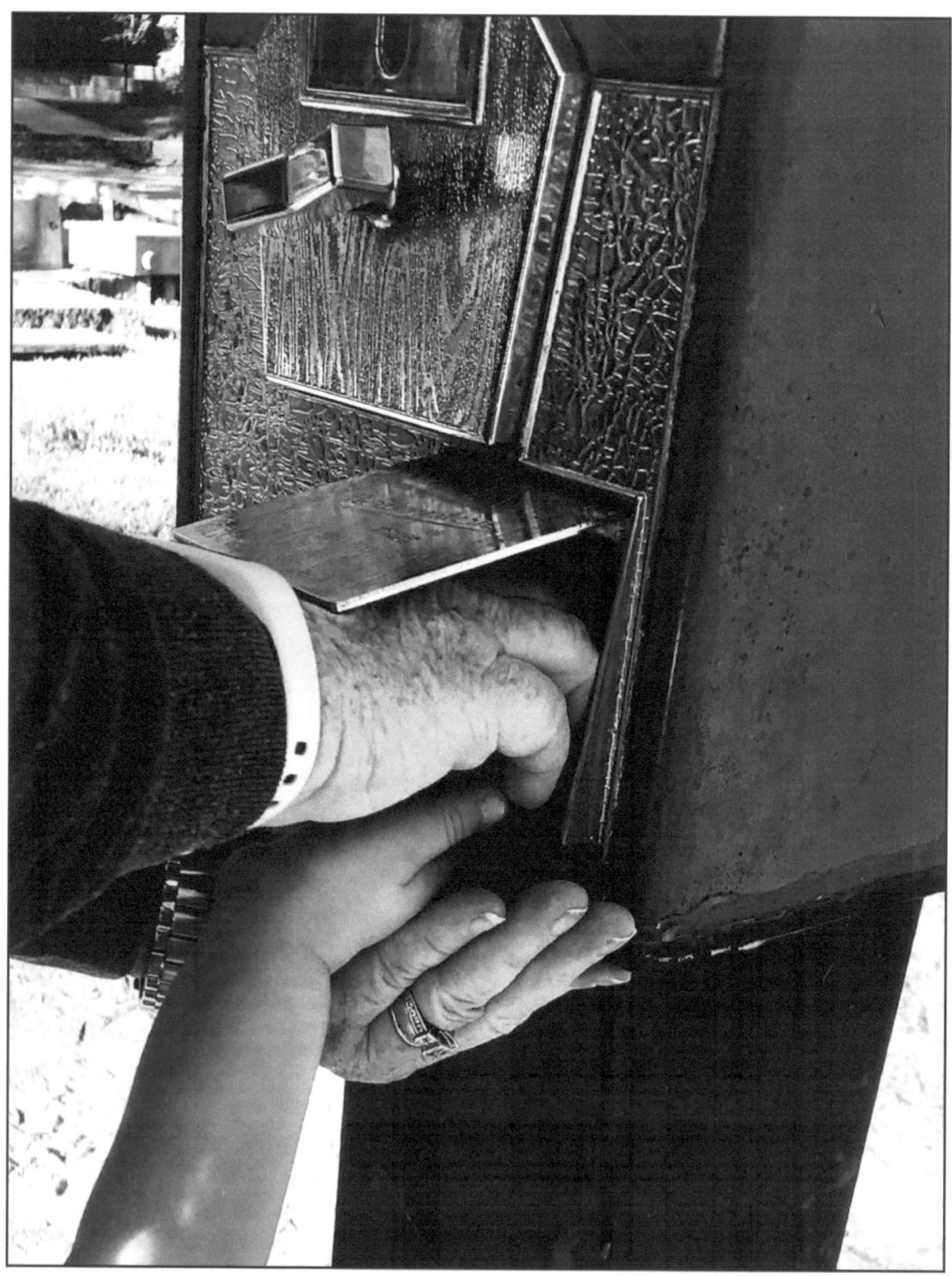

And Here We Are

Laura Iodice

And here you are, such a fine woman.
So far traveled from the little girl
Who sang to the moon
through her bedroom window.
Ariel, afloat at sea.

And here I am, wise too late,
Watching you make your way
From moon to sea, to distant shore,
The tides behind you.
Gaia, your feet solidly rooted in soil.

And there you go, a streak of mercury,
A flash of light. Sure-footed,
You soar across the jet-black sky,
Gravitating
Toward who knows where?

And here I am on steady ground now,
Secure that you will safely land,
No matter the map that guides you,
No matter the sting of rain against your face
As you move so swiftly passed my door.

The UnCorinthian Vow

Laura Johnson

Love is patient and after
one week
the new unsweetened moon saw
you push rocks down my throat
but Love is kind so i
kindly told you
to go directly to hell but
Love does not envy so you invited me
to join you
but i couldn't when i remembered that
Love does not boast even though
you did when you followed me
revealing the others you'd
rather have married and
Love and i are not proud of clouded tempers
but like Love
i was not self-seeking so i shrank
forgetting family
losing friends
abandoning
self
i became like
Love, not easily angered and
i unexisted when you were
two three four hours late
dishes broke
bruises marked
days
Love keeps no record of wrongs but
i did and i gave
it to the lawyer to build a case even though
Love does not delight in evil
 there was plenty of unconfession
father, forgive him for he
has sinned
while Love rejoices in the truth
the two-sided
reconstructed
slightly skewed
court-approved
truth

if Love always protects
it looks out for number one
but still
Love always trusts
when we didn't
and even wading out of crazy
Love hopes for
decent child support and
minimal interruption
to the holidays and

Love

perseveres

but you didn't

and

Love

never fails

but

i do.

apache tears

Jason Hackett

The tears of Apache wives
        wept deep into the mountainside,

Plenty enough to fill
        the white boys' tin buckets –

    plunk, plunk, plunk.

Hold a stone teardrop in your palm
        and you never have to weep again,

It does all the weeping for you,
        legend has it.

Real bones at the base of the cliff,
        warriors too proud to die indignantly,

Now forgotten relics picked over
        in the afterlife,

Unnamed gravestones of shadowy translucence
        caught between eye and sun,

Incur happiness in the innocence
        of not knowing.

The tears' only inclusions,
        mourning, imperfections

Rock tumblers and history books
        can easily spin a shine on –

    plunk, plunk, plunk.

Wanderings

George Stein

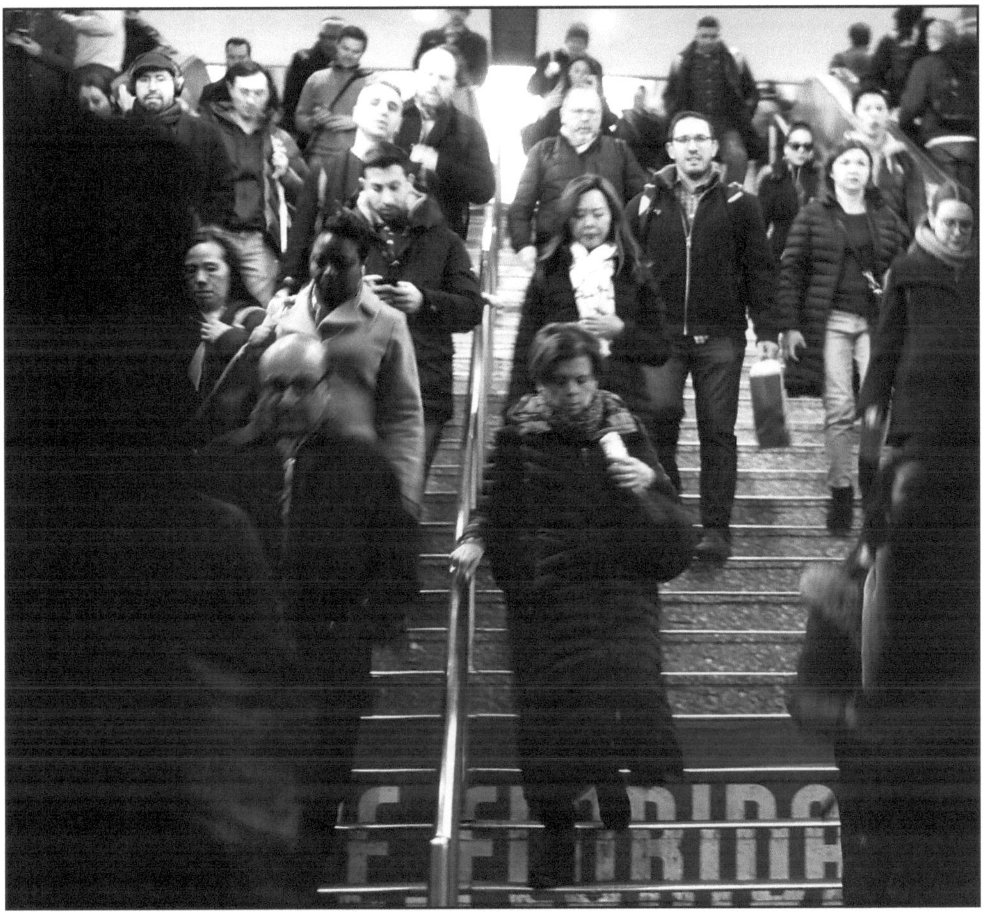

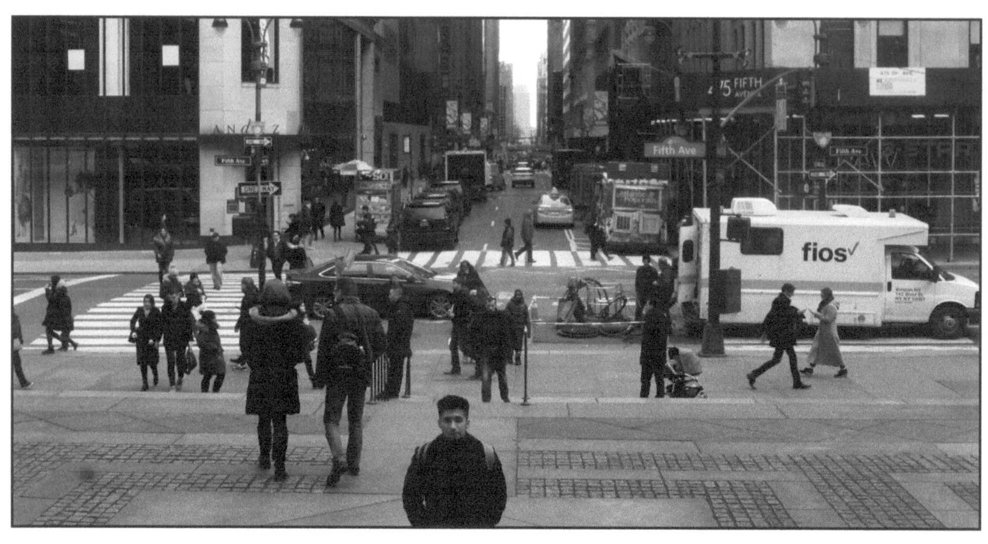

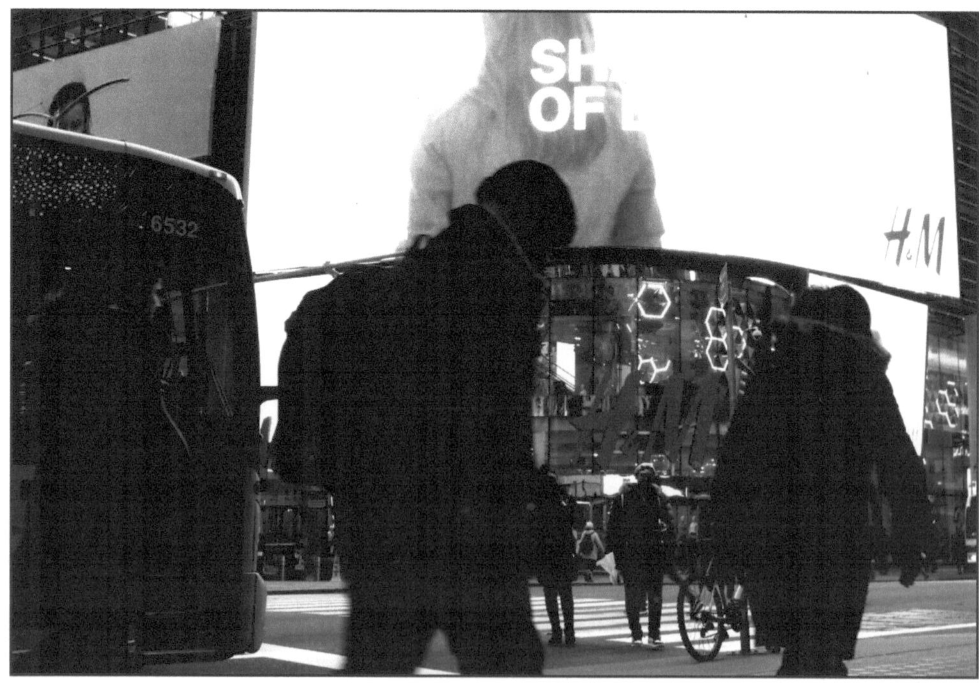
SH
OF
6532
H&M

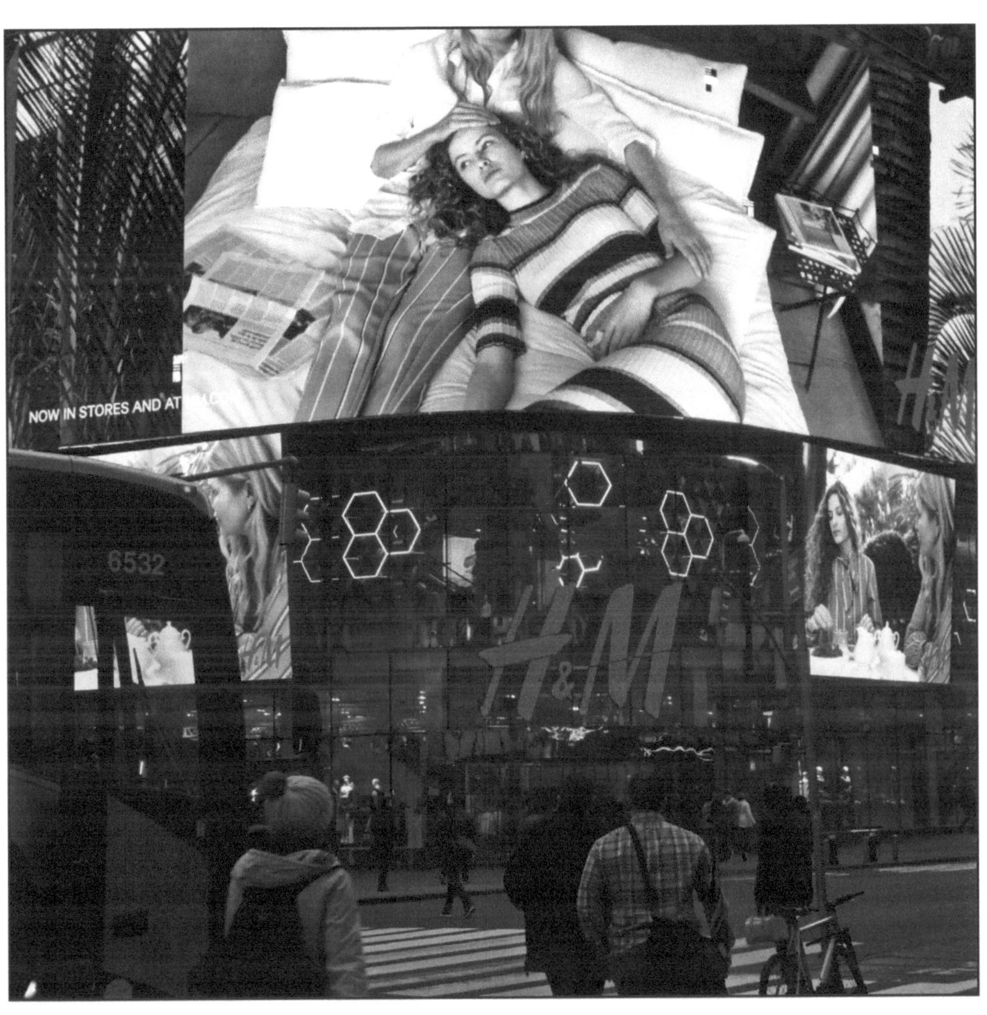

NOW IN STORES AND AT
6532
H&M

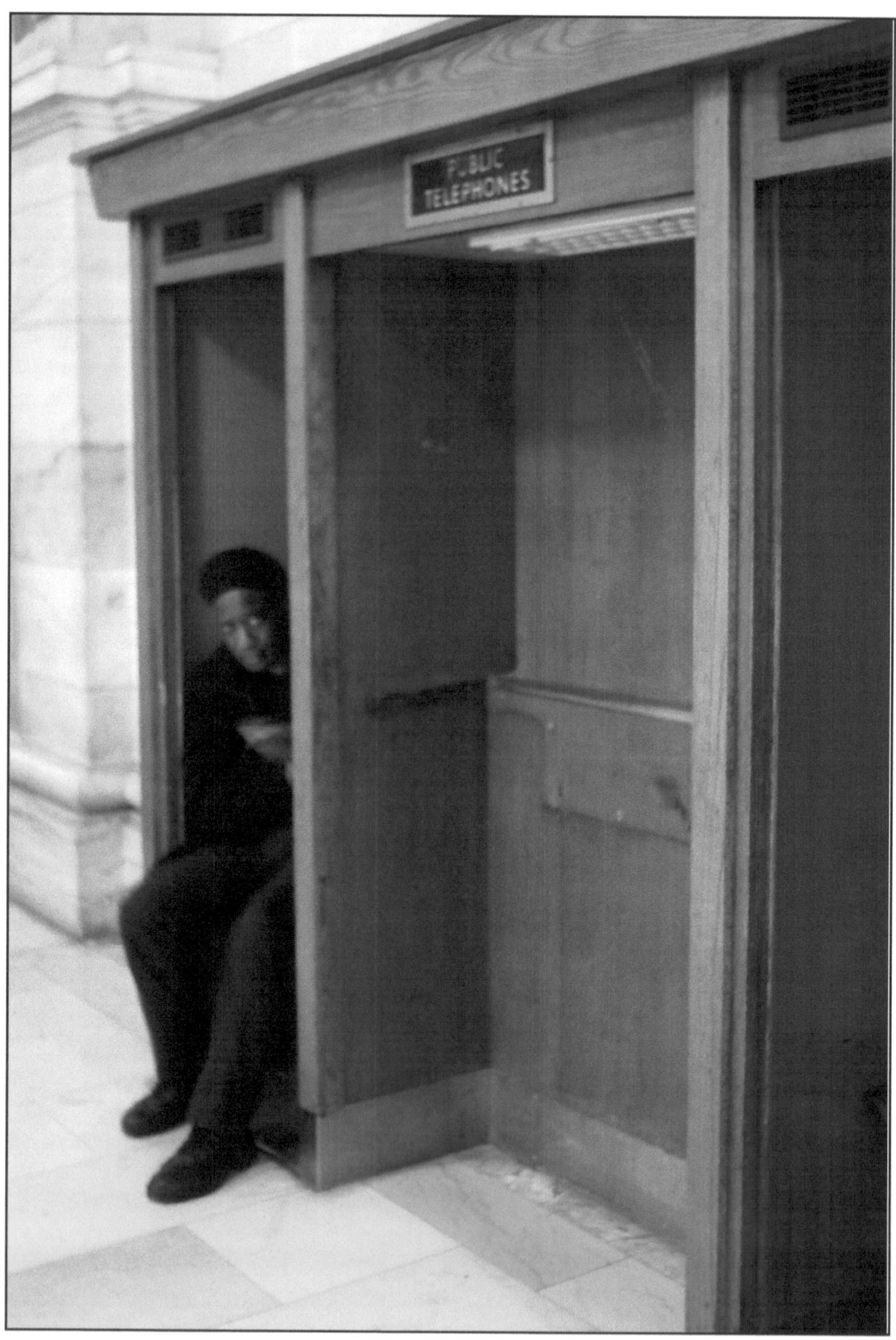
PUBLIC
TELEPHONES

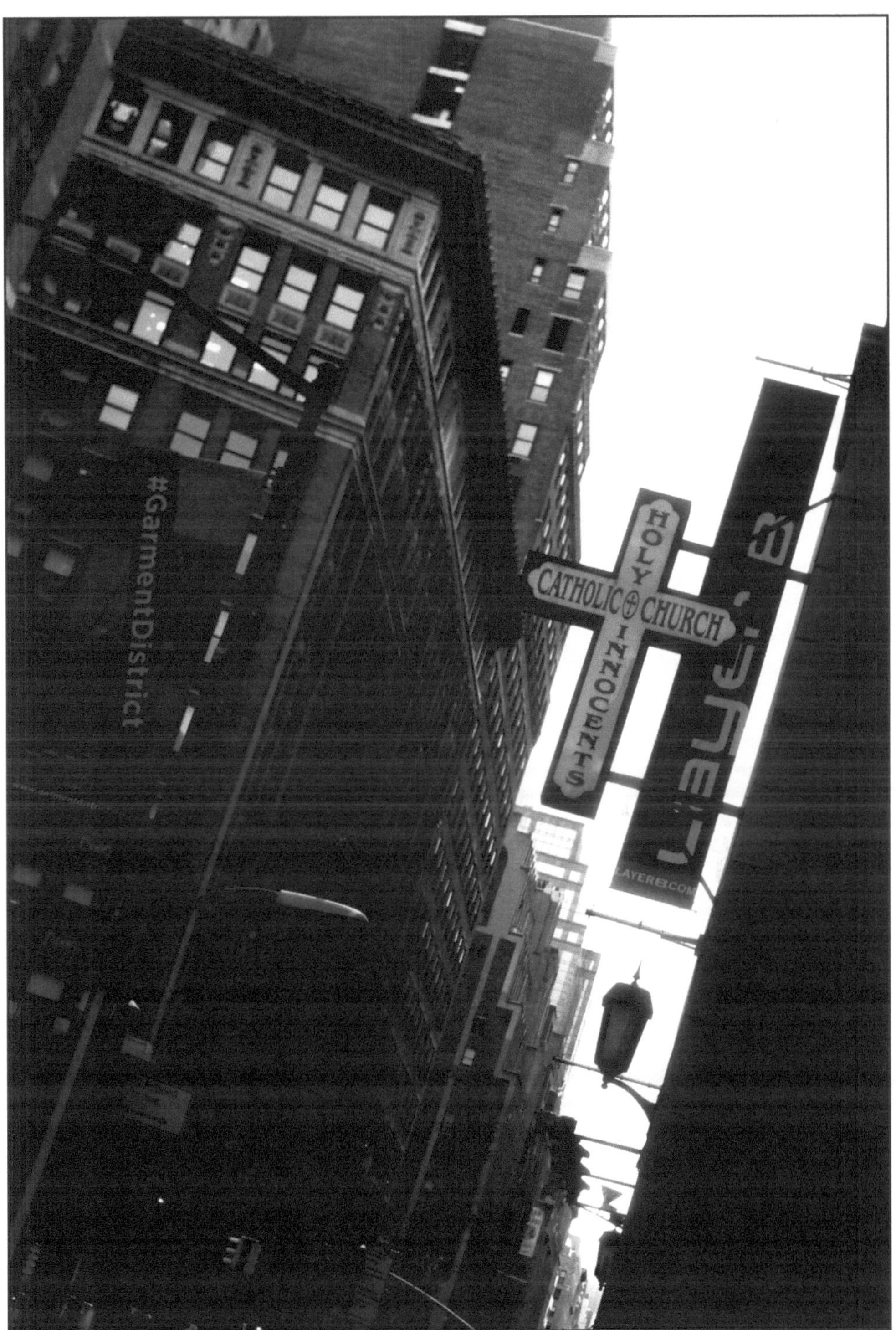

#GarmentDistrict
HOLY INNOCENTS CATHOLIC CHURCH
PLAYERS.COM

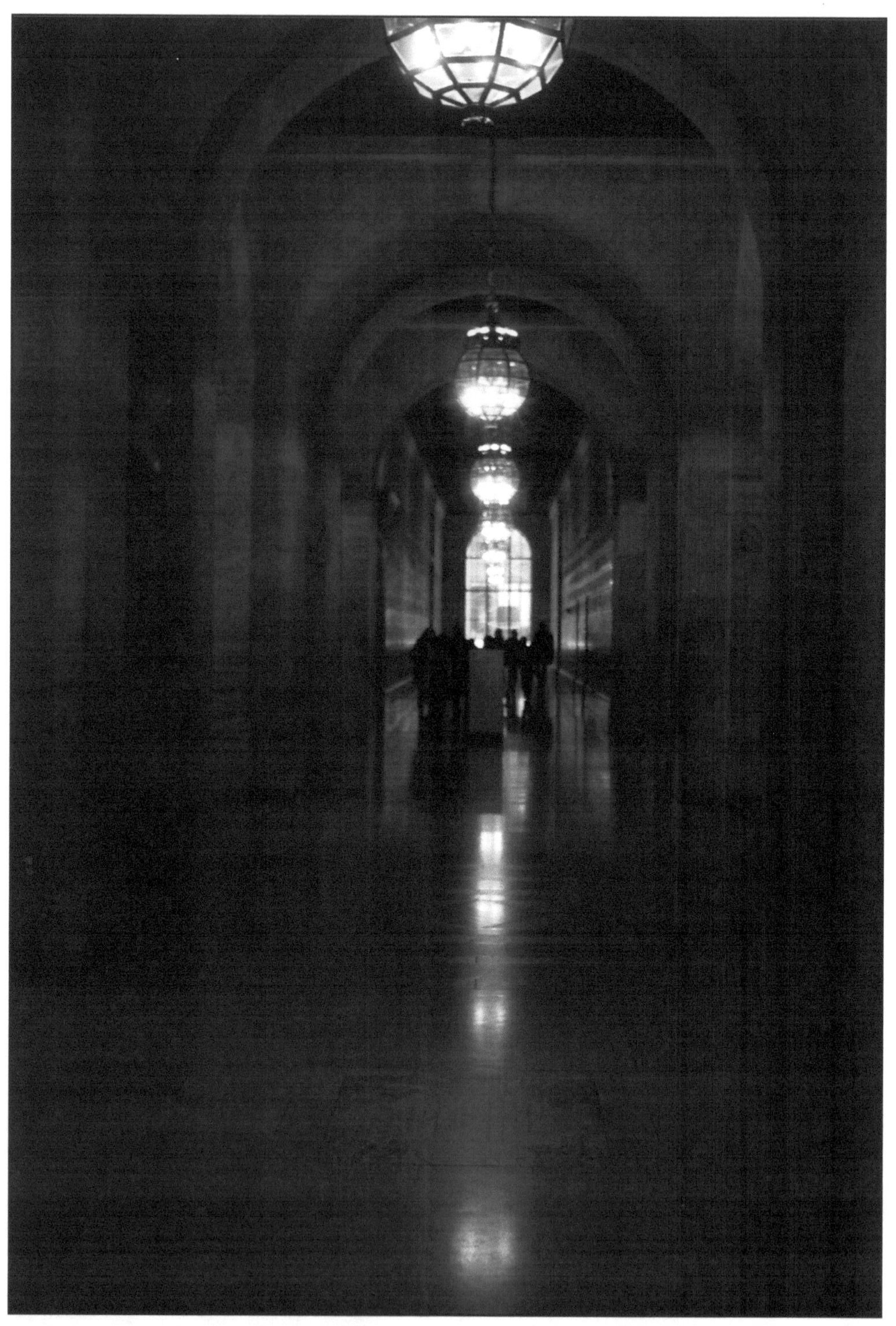

THE NEW YORKER PLIGHT

Saanya Ali

It takes leaving New York to come to terms with how wholeheartedly you believe that anyone who doesn't live in New York is in some way kidding.

Going as far as booking any flight out of Laguardia or JFK or even Newark (if you've got six hours to spare), to register the fact that costumes of unfurrowed brows and content smiles, are more than part of some well-rehearsed performance art piece, and that people can be genuinely happy without recommending the drug, diet, or shrink that caused it.

But they don't get it.

We like our grumpy.

We sprinkle sardonic, and cynical, and sarcastic in our burnt backwash bodega coffee every morning, and order our Resting Bitch Faces™ on Amazon Prime with next day delivery.

Because we can.

We can eat pizza at 4am and not care about the calories because they don't count if you don't count 'em.
We can point to our fire escapes and diners and ex-best friend's therapists offices in the background of every sit-com, rom com, and nighttime news broadcast because we're just that important.
We can curse out slow walkers because we know there are no roses to stop and smell here.
And we can bump into every person we forgot we went to high school with, during intern season, and stand taller because every bouncer knows us by name and now we have the upper hand despite being called Frizzy for the better part of four years.

No, anyone who doesn't live in New York doesn't understand what it's like to consider human sacrifice for a washer/dryer in unit and to think carefully about offering up one's first born for a security deposit. Like being a fat child or bullied as a prepubescent, these are the things that build character, and we don't take anyone without character here. You can just check your bags at the tunnel and settle in Jersey if you're the type to hesitate when crossing the street because some public art piece flashes an orange hand symbolically.

If you make it here, you learn certain things.

You know that your whole day is blessed if you get to the station right when the J arrives because another just isn't coming.
You know that you never want to see the ball drop on New Years because it's painfully underwhelming.

You know that you've got superpowers (or a really short skirt) if you can get a cab in midtown in the rain.

You know that every July you'll have your Pantene commercial moment at least twice a day when the train enters the station and the recycled burp of air that follows it dries the sweat from your hair.

And you know that you will forever feel like you're in a fairytale if you're wearing shoes that click against the marble in the main hall of the Public Library at Bryant Park.

It just doesn't make sense how anyone can live anywhere without a steady supply of deli bagels to get through the day?

Take any given Saturday—
You're sitting at a bar, making small talk with Brad, the quarterback brunette, trying to be a comedian, who tore his ACL, hiking the Appalachians with his dad and dog, both named Mark, just sipping your drink, when he mentions something about being from Dallas, or Chicago, or San Diego, or this quaint little town off then coast of irrelevant. He's kinda cute, but Brad is no bridge and tunnel commuter that qualifies as close enough if it's late enough and you're lonely enough.

You've just got to stare into those farmer boy blue eyes and convince yourself that Brad's just really bad at comic delivery, and Mark and Marsha were right when they said he should've become an accountant like his brother, and wait for the punchline. But after the most painful kidney stone of silence passes, he smiles, and you're sure it's because the memory of your overpriced salad has taken residence between your teeth, but it's not.

He was serious.

The grin that continues to be slathered across his Wonder Bread face isn't mocking but...genuine? And you're just a heartless asshole rudely staring at a stranger in a bar. Because when you leave New York, it's impolite to stare or to point. To barrel directly into unassuming strangers or to decidedly look through a person with a clipboard on the street.

No. There's no getting out of this one.

Instead, you have to transfigure your grimace into a smile (the way one might for a child delivering an impassioned monologue about Santa Clause) then say something like, "Oh yes, I hear the rhubarb jam in North I Couldn't Care Less is lovely this time of year," in order to gracefully extract yourself from his delusions, and pray that he comes to his senses eventually.

But honestly, New York doesn't have space for Brad, or anyone like him who doesn't acknowledge that the rats on the L platform and the bodega cats on 6th are our shared custody pets or who knows when a rhubarb's blooming season is (unless they're the Sous Chef at Per Se).

When you live anywhere else, how do you decide which friends you want to stay in touch with if you can't rule out the outer burrow boys who don't live on your line or the Thursday night friends who live in a six floor walk up?

How do you reason that the only friends that you need to get Christmas presents for are the ones that will remember you did in August when they're the only ones with a working AC?

What do you do in the shower if not think about witty comebacks to the cat-callers on Stanton that you've come to expect and worry about when missing?

What do you get the homeless man on Broadway if you don't know his exact coffee specifications?

Who would you have a stimulating book club with if not the eighty year old men who never left The Village?

I just don't get it.

So next time you want to pick free french fries off my plate at Veselka (because family doesn't pay), just know that this is the only city that makes any sense. Now hush, while I complain about climbing my seven story walk up with five Whole Foods bags but continue to pay two hundred dollars a month for an Equinox membership.

Tenure-Track Survival Tips for Female Assistant Professors

Eryn O'Neal

1. Never turn down an invitation to collaborate, even if it means you'll be exploited, underpaid, and treated like a graduate student. It's still a great opportunity.

2. Join as many committees as you can. Join university committees. Join department committees. Join standing committees. Join subcommittees. Join ad hoc committees. Committees. Committees. Committees.

3. Regarding item #2, never disagree with white-straight-male colleagues on key committee votes. Whenever possible, vote in agreement. Abstention is almost as controversial as voting against.

4. Be likable. Please everyone. Collegiality counts.

5. Ignore misogynistic comments; better yet, laugh at them. If a colleague asks you if they can say something sexist, always answer in the affirmative.

6. Dress business-sexy, but demure. Think sexy librarian without the self-confidence.

7. Never voice your opinions during faculty meetings, college meetings, lunch meetings, coffee meetings, hallway meetings, or doorway-lingering meetings. In fact, never let anyone hear you speak.

8. Smile—always.

9. Don't correct people when they refer to you as Mrs., Ms., or Miss. Doctorate or not, it comes across as stuck-up.

10. Mentor triple the amount of graduate students compared to your male colleagues.

11. Keep your head down (e.g., when walking, taking, and teaching; during office hours, meetings, and university events; in every situation, really).

12. If you think you're doing enough university and department service, quadruple it.

13. Be authoritarian, enthusiastic, bubbly, and cold in the classroom.

14. Spend 2 hours a day reading about or talking about work/life balance.

15. Spend 2 hours a day reading about or talking about impostor syndrome.

16. Advise at least one student organization or club. Bonus if the club meets late in the evening. This item is especially true for the young, unmarried, and child-free.

17. Play golf. Most importantly, look cute doing it.

18. Eliminate "no" from your vocabulary.

19. Don't forget about your research. Weekends, evenings, holidays, vacations, weddings, and funerals provide the perfect opportunities to get your writing done.

20. Do it all. Still, do more.

The Catering Service on the Mount

Robert Morella

32 AD, Somewhere in Northern Israel

Dusty and hot, Sol McSolomon thought to himself, no wonder his restaurant was always so empty. It was a slow and hot afternoon at Sol's Restaurant as usual. The heat of northern Israel was not his friend. Although he owned the restaurant, he was also the chef, the waiter, and the one who swept the floor. He leaned on his broom and let out a sigh. Despite being close to the Sea of Galilee, the restaurant was simply too dusty and hot.

Suddenly the phone rang. Sol sprang from his seat and answered on the first ring.

"Sol's catering, Sol speaking. How can I brighten your day?" he said.

"Sol, it's Jesus, I hope I caught you at a good time," He said.

"For you Jesus, it's always a good time. Remember you cured my blindness. I was blind as a...what do you call those things?" he said.

"Bats," Jesus said.

"Bats, I was blind as a freaking bat and you fixed it, so I owe you big time," he said.

"Don't mention it," said Jesus, "I'm glad to help out when I can."

There was a long pause, then Jesus cleared his throat.

 "Um, Sol, the reason I called is that we've got a huge freaking problem," He continued, "we got the bread and fish you sent earlier—those were great by the way—but we have a huge problem."

"Jesus, what kind of problem?" he said, "was the food okay?"

"Well here's the deal—we made a mistake—maybe we printed *too many flyers* for the event. As it turns out we have a *lot* more people than we expected. Can you do me a solid and send over more of your most excellent bread and fish?" He said.

"Sure Jesus, anything for a good customer. What do you need?" he said.

"We need a LOT," Jesus said.

"No problem," Sol said, "how many portions?"

"Five thousand and twelve," He said.

There was a long silence on the phone.

"Jesus, is this one of those prank calls they put on the radio? I mean, Jesus Christ, we *do* get a lot of those!" he said. "No, I'm serious bro, it's no prank—my dad taught me better than to do something like that," He said.

"Okay, give me a minute to add up what its gonna cost," he said.

"Um Sol, I was kinda hoping you would comp this food. Trust me this would be *great* publicity. I've got a *sweet* book deal and…"

Interrupting, "Comp? As in FREE?" he said, his voice rising, "*Jesus H. Christ*, you want five thousand freaking portions of fish and bread for FREE? I don't run a charity here! I don't give a rat's ass about your friggin book deal! Call me back when you want to pay!" he said.

The phone line went dead.

"Hello, Sol? Hello?" He said, but was met with silence.

Jesus wept.

He put down the phone and felt dejected. There was only one other catering company in the region and he hoped he would have better luck with them. Jesus picked up the phone and dialed the number.

Love and Other Apertures

Art by Nathan Holloway
Poem by Abigail McFee

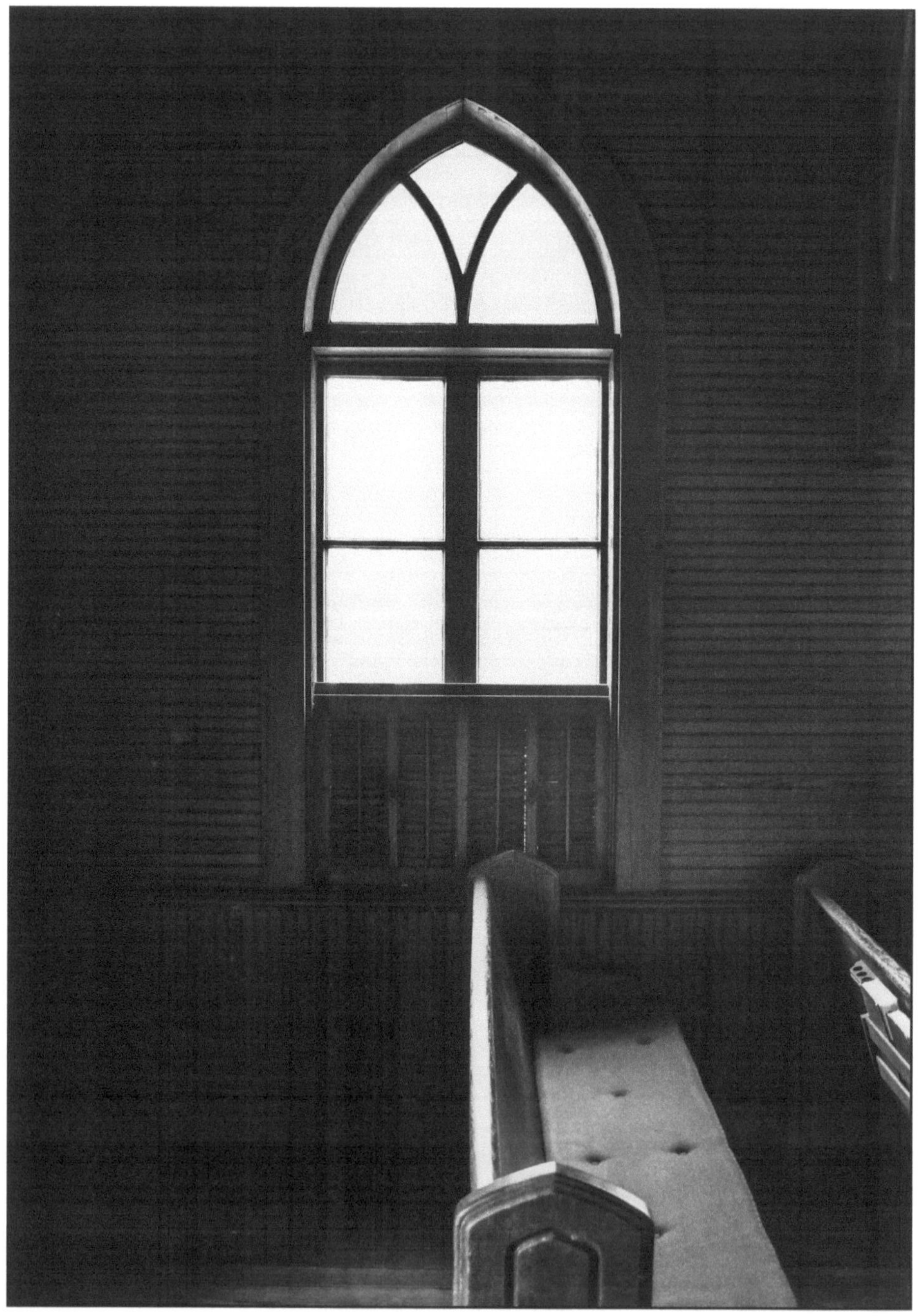

Window petaled to the wall,
finding union

in a sharp arch—lancet,

a knife that slices through tendons
and tissue. A man I leaned my body into

went to church as fingers go
curiously to a wound. I came along

as a person comes into love,

architectural ache for substance
and space, windows

and walls. When he held the hymnal open
for me, the thin pages parted

slickly. I opened,

whose interest was not in God
but proximity,

how he sang softly

into the space between our bodies.

Hearing what was held
in the organ's swell, not

the thud of leather as the last-
lifted note snaps shut, I stayed

until the pews were empty. Stared at the window,
seeing not lancet

but light paring open,

parting us.

In Order Of Appearance:

Andreas Fleps is a 27-year-old poet, based near Chicago. He has a degree in Theology, where he also studied Philosophy. He translates teardrops.

Brynn is a transgender poet. Her work has appeared in Iowa's Best Emerging Poets, Go Magazine, INK LIT MAG, The Paha Review, Little Village Magazine. She is currently pursuing her M.F.A. from Sarah Lawrence College. You can find her @brynnfest on twitter and at brynnbogert.com

Christine Alexander is a creative writing major at Southern New Hampshire University. Her work has appeared in Barren Magazine and The Penmen Review. She lives in Gloucester, MA.

Kevin Edwards is an interdisciplinary artist and musician whose artwork is inseparable from music. Edwards imagery breaks music down to its essential forms and then reforms it in a visual space, a conscious attempt to convey the important emotional association of the audible world to the visual.

Alison Lubar (formerly Myers) teaches high school English by day and yoga by night. She lives in New Jersey, with a bad dog and an overgrown garden. Her work has been published by SWWIM Every Day, trampset, The Esthetic Apostle, Lady Blue Literary Arts Journal, Cathexis Northwest Press, and in great weather for MEDIA's most recent anthology, Suitcase of Chrysanthemums; she also has a piece forthcoming in Glassworks. Follow her on Twitter @theoriginalison

Ginny Short is a graduate of the Regis University Mile High MFA program in Denver, CO, with a specialization in poetry and creative non-fiction. She is an arid land ecologist working for a non-profit in the field of conservation. These wild and beautiful landscapes provide ample inspiration for her writing. She has had poems published in the 2018 Anthology "Fire and Rain: Ecopoetry of California," Minerva Rising, Cholla Needles Press, Mojave River Review, Mojave He[art] Review, The Avocet, Plum Tree Tavern and Silver Birch Press, Ribbons and others. She is working on her first book. www.ginnyshort.com.

Violet Knight is a young transgender poet and law student living in Englewood, Colorado. She's a proud Winthrop University alumna, collector of college t-shirts, and has also been featured in the Spring 2019 issue of The Oakland Review.

Born in Coshocton, OH, Matt Gold is based in Brooklyn, NY, where he divides his time between music and photography. As evidence of the democratizing nature of his approach to photography, Gold has no formal training in the visual arts. His first image, a picture of his cat on a Sony Ericsson Z310A flip phone, was taken in 2008, and he has continued to explore the aesthetic possibilities of that instrument, resisting the updated phones and apps available and revealing a contemporary nostalgia that encompasses the prolific imagery of our visual culture. Gold's work has been featured in numerous publications and journals.

Paul Iasevoli's stories and poems have been published in various journals, including Deep South Magazine, where he was 2018 winner of honorable mention. His writing has also appeared in the Florida Writers Association's yearly collection of prose and poetry. He's author of the 2018 award nominated LGBTQ+ novella, Winter Blossoms.

Riley Fields is a twenty something living on Long Island in New York. She writes free verse poetry and prose, and believes that healing is an art that deserves to be shared.

A native of Philadelphia, Pennsylvania, Planta's creative background includes study at the renowned Judimar School of Dance and classical piano instruction at the Curtis School of Music. Her visual arts studies were ensued and completed at The Tyler School of Art and Maryland Institute College of Art. Awards include the D.C. Commission on the Arts Artist Residency program, the American Association of University Womens' career grant and Philadelphia Ethical Society Emerging Artist Award. Musically, with a style that has been described as "distinctively original", Planta has performed, recorded, regionally and, choreographed a variety of stage productions, including, The Takoma Park Youth Theatre Players and The Hart Dance Ensemble. Her art has been featured in solo and group art exhibitions nationally as well.

Kathryn Schwartz is a mediocre political science student studying at Smith College in Massachusetts. She thoroughly believes poetry and the power of citrus.

Kayla Branstetter is a mother, educator, writer, and artist who holds a Master of Arts in Liberal Studies degree in art, literature, and culture from the University of Denver. Her writing and photography were published in Ozark Hills and Hollows, a regional magazine focusing on local culture. In the past, her poem, "The Dollar" was published in bordertown, a literary journal for Missouri Southern State University. Recently, her creative nonfiction piece, "Graduation," was published in the Fredericksburg Literary and Art Review in June of 2018. Her art collection, "Silent Spring Awakens", was published in The Esthetic Apostle in May of 2018, her art collection "Excuse Me" was published in the gyara journal, and my art piece, "Grandma's Garden" was published in From Whisper to Roar. Her art piece, "Innocence" was part of the "My American Internment" an online exhibit and on tour for the North Dakota Human Rights Festival sponsored by the Human Family. her art piece "Life's Dance" was a part of the Light Space & Time Online Gallery--8th Annual All Women Online Art Competition. Recently, her creative nonfiction piece, "Grief," and black and white photograph, "Haunted Hotel" was published in the Crowder Quill.

Laura Iodice, a Bronx native, has resided with her husband in Syracuse, N.Y. for the past forty years. She is a veteran secondary and post-secondary educator, has taught classes in literature, composition, rhetoric and cultural constructions of race and has published professionally about these subjects. Her creative non-fiction is featured in the literary journals Conclave Magazine, The Write Launch, Litro, Metafore Magazine, Crack the Spine and Vending Machine Press. Teaching is her vocation; writing is her life.

Laura Johnson is poet in Eastern Iowa who serves as co-editor of the online literary journal Backchannels. Laura is a graduate (BA '89, MA '92) of the University of Iowa. She participates regularly in performance and slam poetry, as well as writing page poetry. Her work has appeared or is forthcoming in Down in the Dirt and Rosebud. In addition to being a poet, Laura leads writing workshops in her community.

Jason Hackett is a small business owner, father of four and sleep deprived. His poems can be found in The Journal of American Poetry, Slippery Elm Literary Journal, Scarlet Leaf Review, Cholla Needles, Crack the Spine, Mental Papercuts, Blue River Review and Sky Island Journal.

George L Stein is a writer and photographer living in Michigan City in Northwest Indiana. George works in both film and digital formats in the urban decay, architecture, fetish, and street photography genres. His emphasis is on composition with the juxtaposition of beauty and decay lying at the center of his aesthetic. Northwest Indiana's rust-belt legacy provides ample locations for industrial backdrops. George has been published in Midwestern Gothic, Gravel, Foliate Oak, After Hours, Hoosier Lit, Gulf Stream Magazine, 3Elements, Stoneboat, Occulum, the Gnu Journal, Iliinot Review and Darkside Magazine.

Saanya Ali is a writer, photographer, and filmmaker. Born in Switzerland, to South Asian parents, growing up in the United States, and traveling to over 50 countries in her first 22 years, she grew up watching the world through airplane windows. Years later, living in New York, she continues to watch the world, now through a different lens. Her cross cultural background and unbridled curiosity continues to inform all that she does and creates. Her fascination with people, places, and travel as well as her desire to tell stories has magnified ten-fold. She loves to take pictures of people in their element, seeking to capture images that reflect the thoughts, emotions, and experiences of the subject at the moment in time at which they cross paths. As a writer and a filmmaker, she hopes to develop these stories through various other mediums including poetry, prose, and both comedic and dramatic dialogue.
A graduate from NYU's Gallatin School of Individualized Study with a concentration in Mixed Media Storytelling, Photography, and Film, she has worked on over a dozen short films and music videos, TV shows including NBC's Blindspot, photographed events for Twitter and red carpets for SxSW, and worked on the social media team for Webby Award winning start up, Well&Good.

Eryn Nicole O'Neal is a criminologist and emerging creative writer who has published research in a variety of scholarly journals, including Justice Quarterly, Violence Against Women, and Journal of Interpersonal Violence. She has one forthcoming fiction short story in DUM DUM, a Los Angeles-based literary magazine named L.A.'s "cult favorite" indie press by The Los Angeles Times. Eryn is an assistant professor in the Department of Criminal Justice and Criminology at Sam Houston State University. Her primary area of research focuses on institutional responses to sexual victimization. She has received six national awards for her research contributions to the study of gender and crime.

Robert Morella is an IT guru from Atlanta, Georgia and also a part-time college professor.

Nathan Holloway is a poet, photographer, and composition instructor living in rural Arkansas and documenting the experience of being rural, queer, and southern. You can find his work in The Esthetic Apostle, GASHER, or on Twitter @unnatural_state.

Abigail McFee is a poet and Nebraska transplant living in Somerville, Massachusetts. She works as editor-in-chief of the Tufts Admissions magazine and formerly wrote an arts column called "Advice from Dead Poets (and Some Living)." You can find her on Twitter @abigail_mcfee.

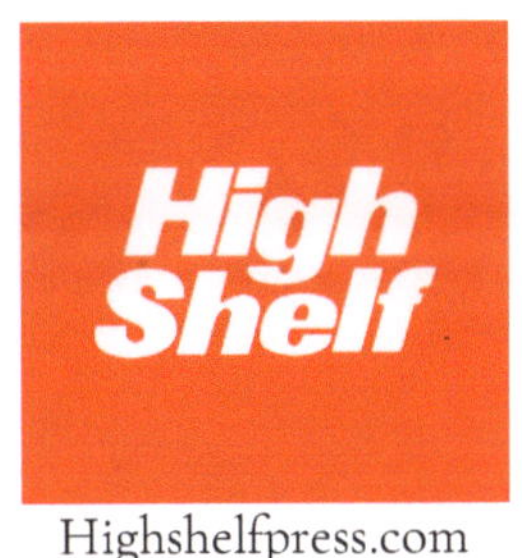

Highshelfpress.com